SNAKE COLORING BOOK

CRYSTAL
COLORING BOOKS

ISBN-13: 978-1547172276
ISBN-10: 1547172274

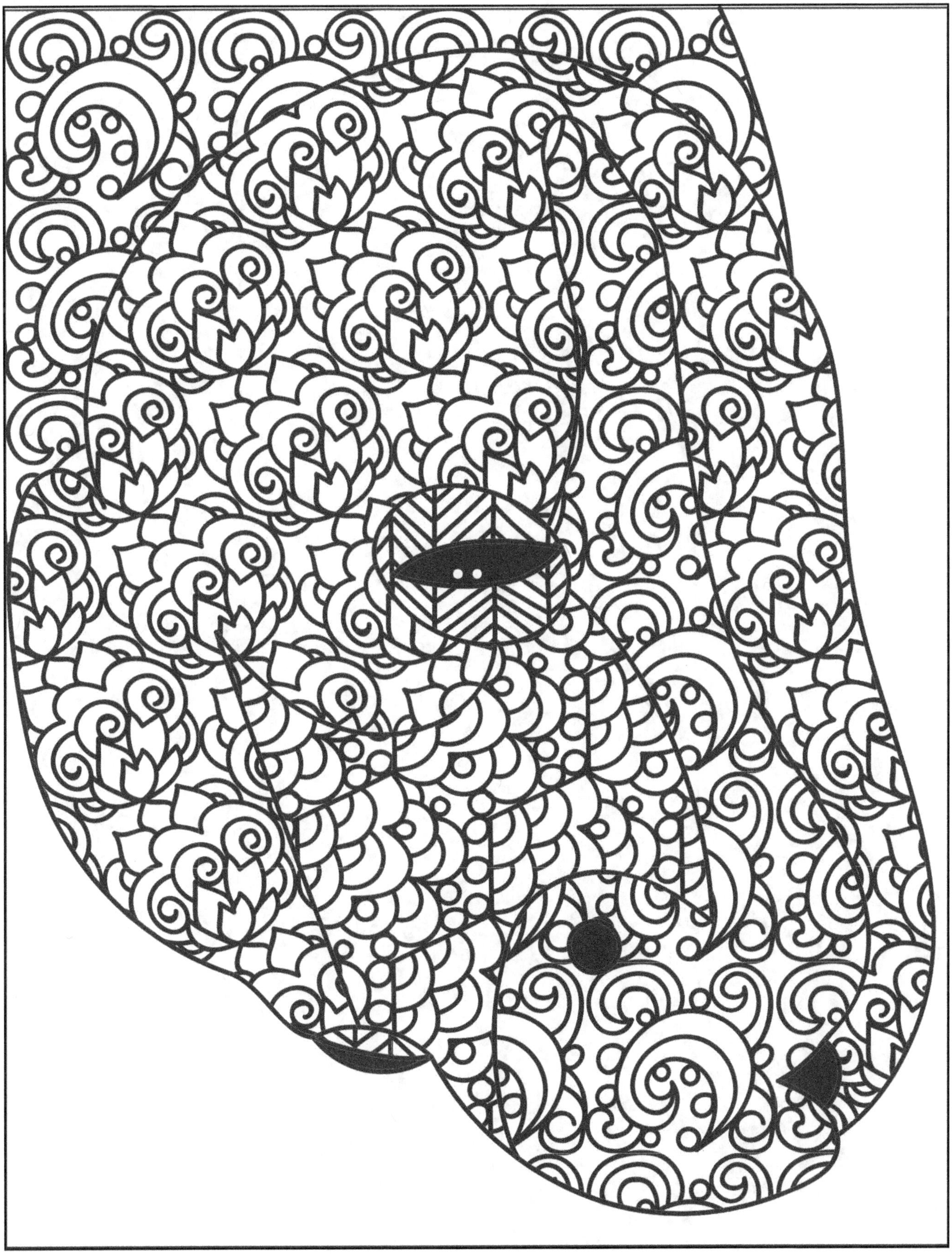

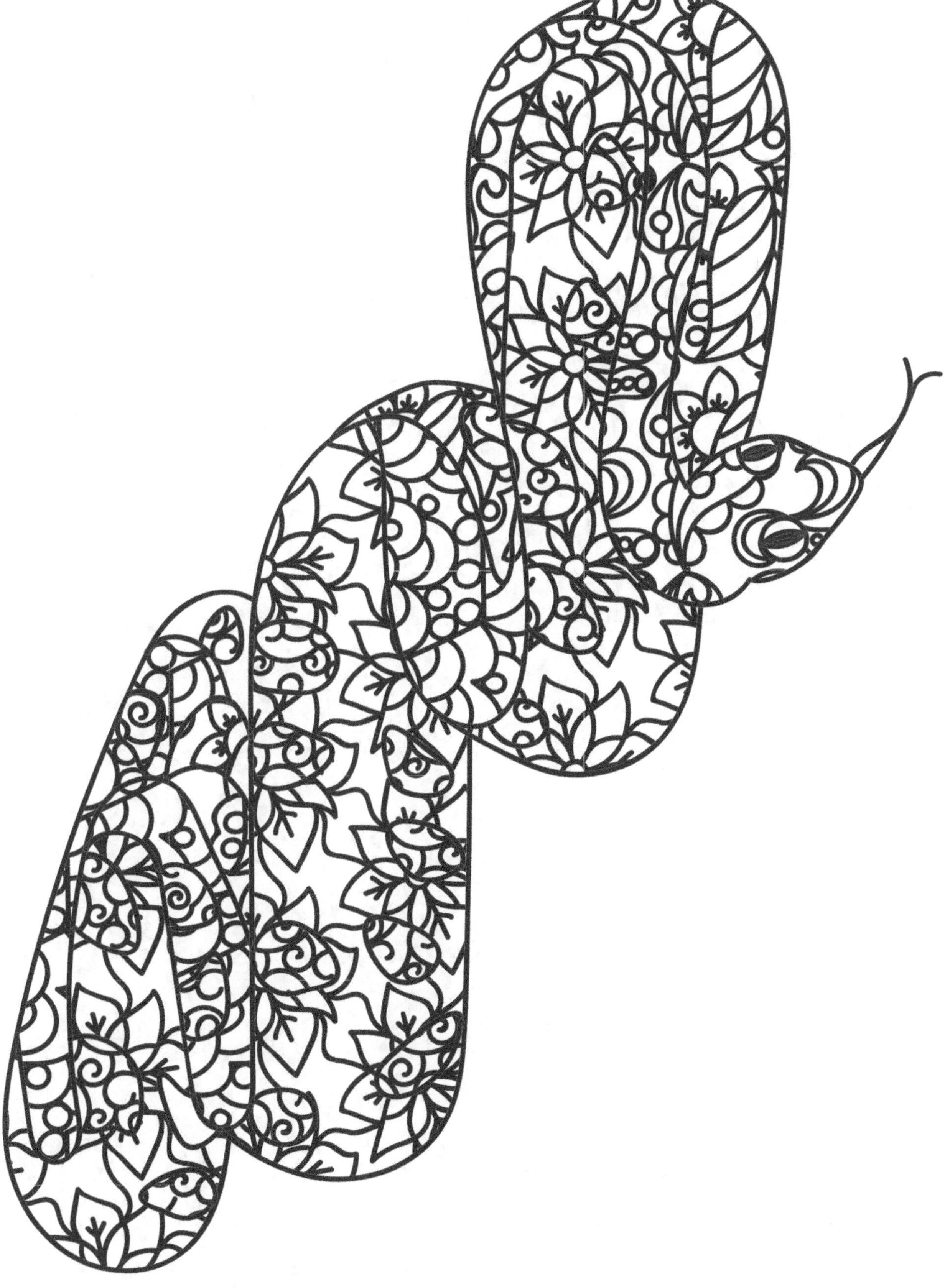

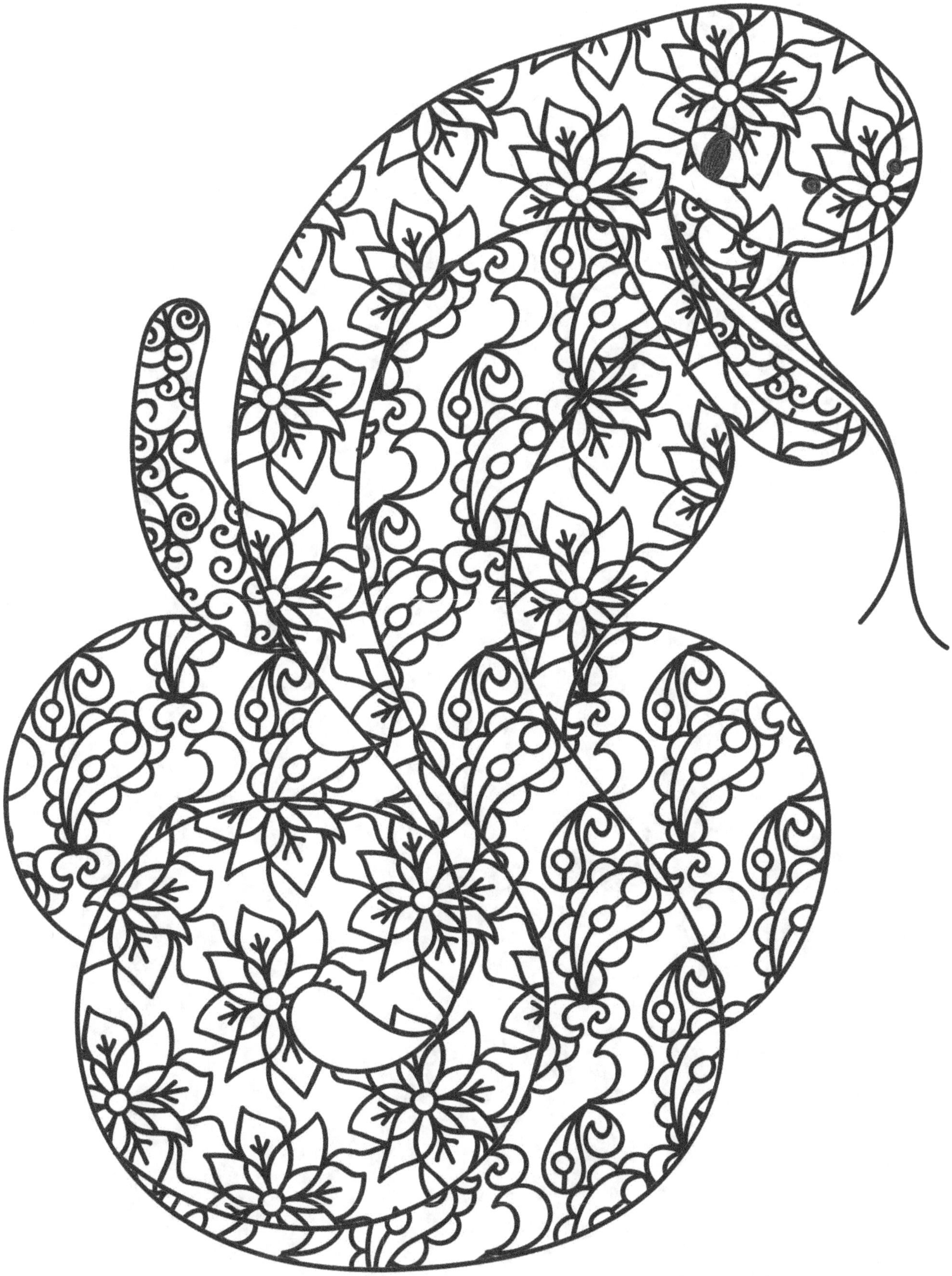

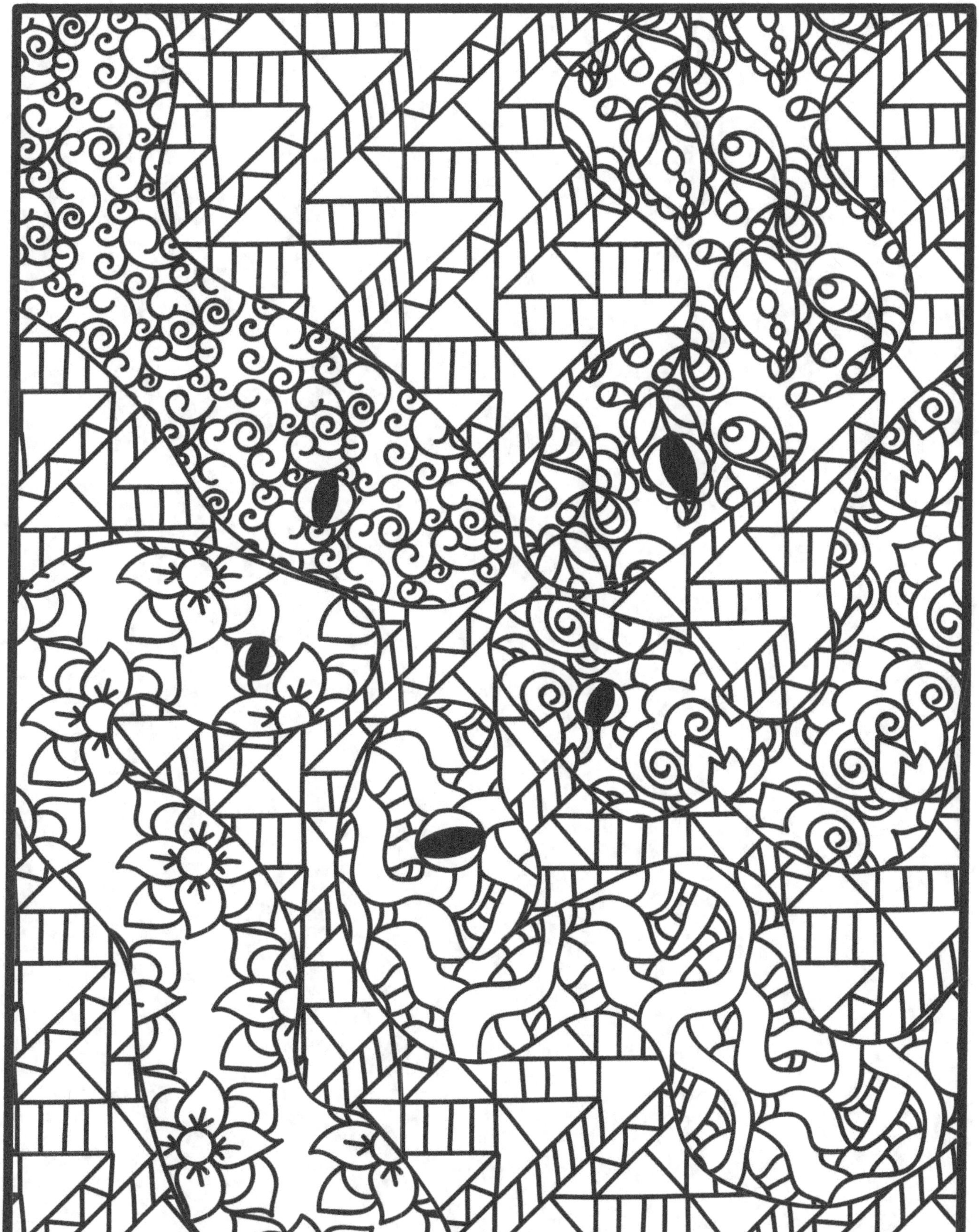

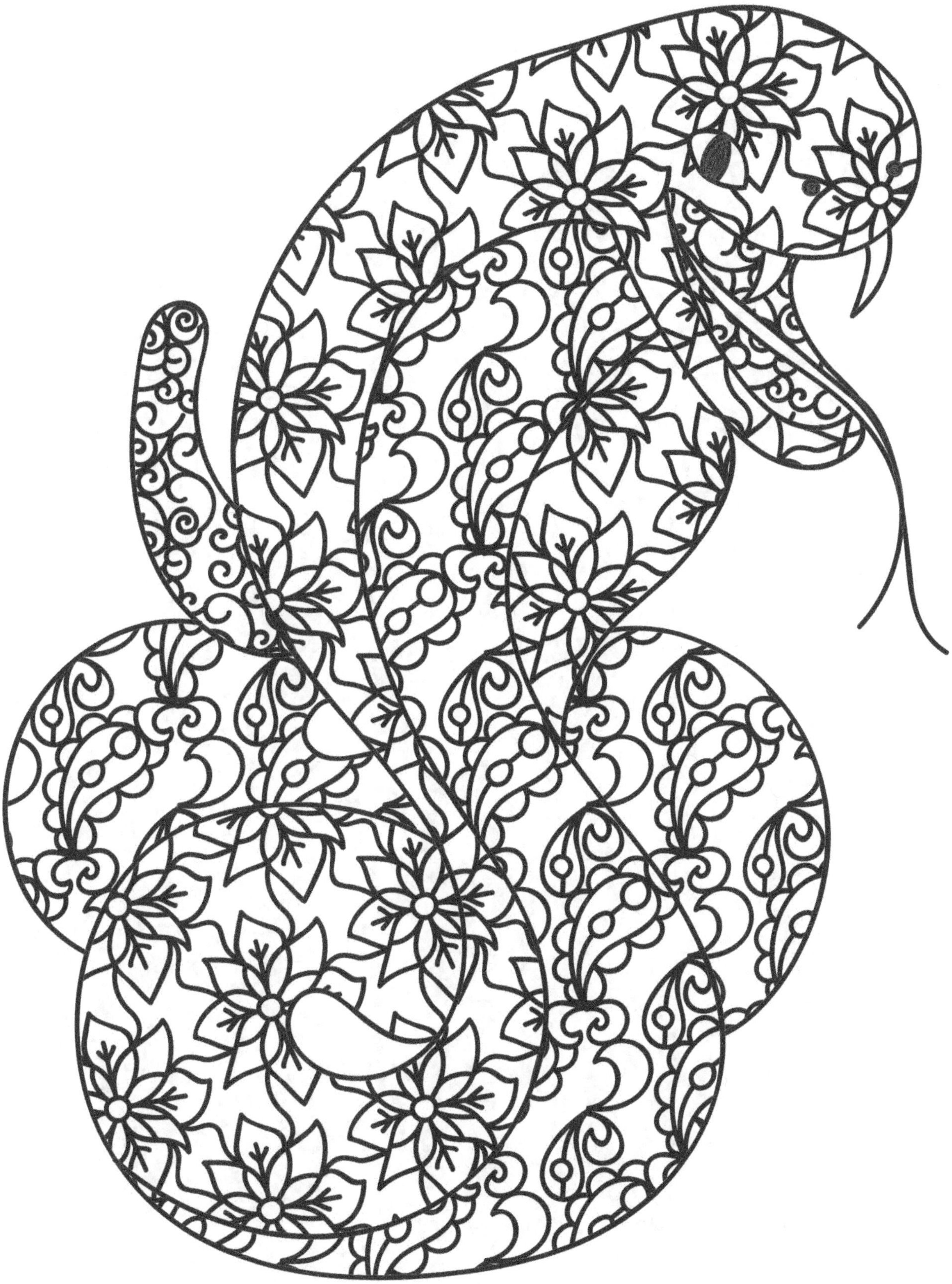

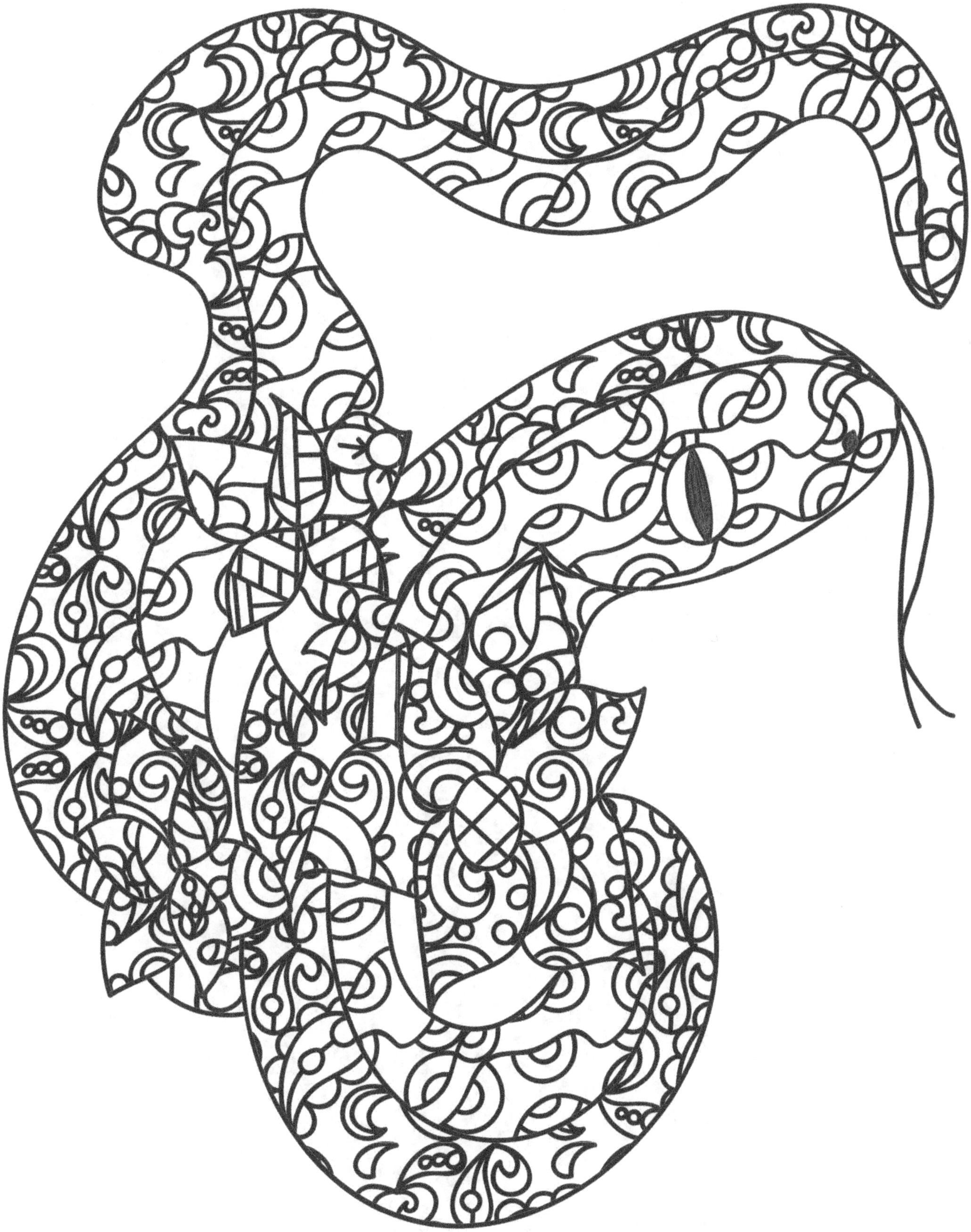

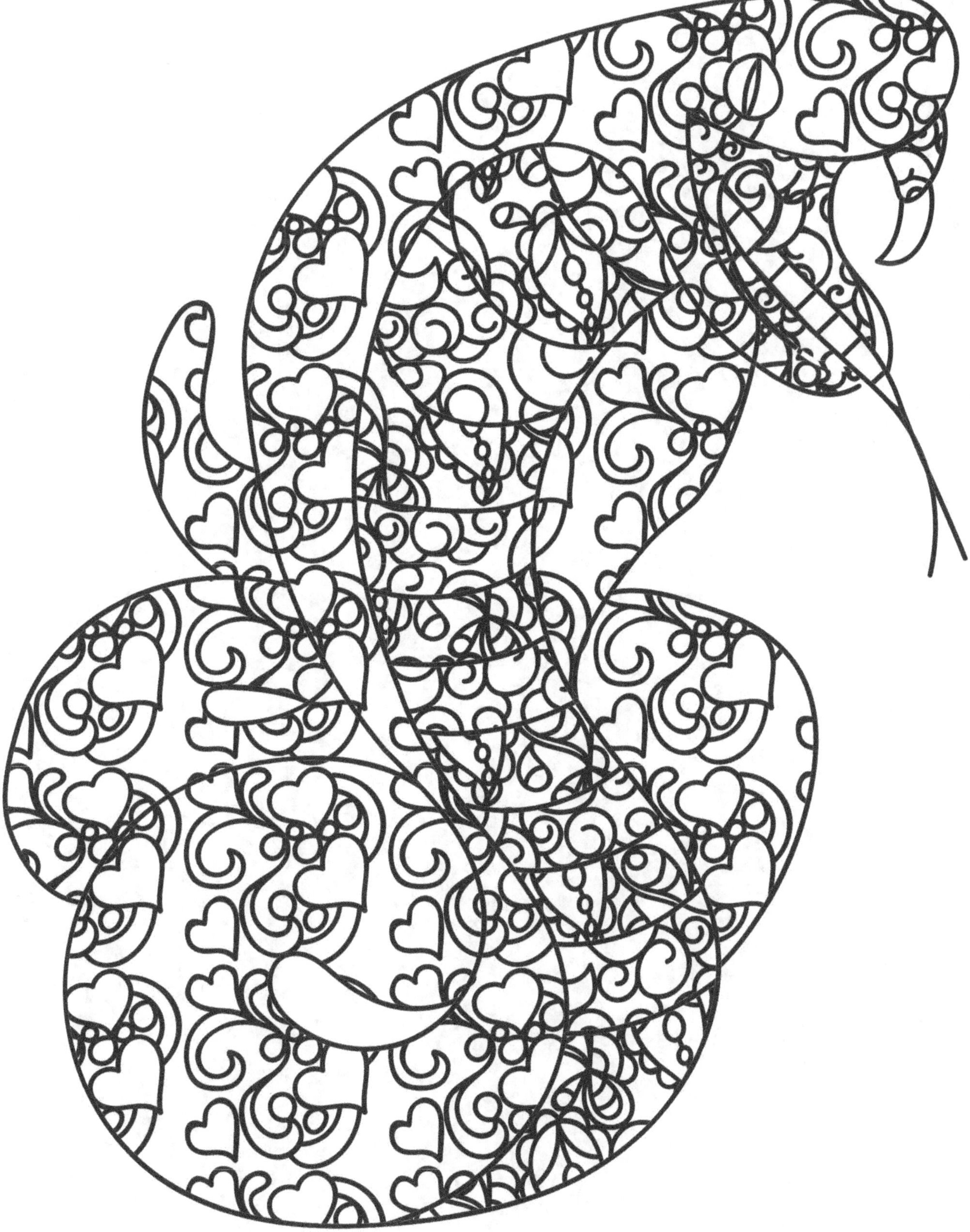

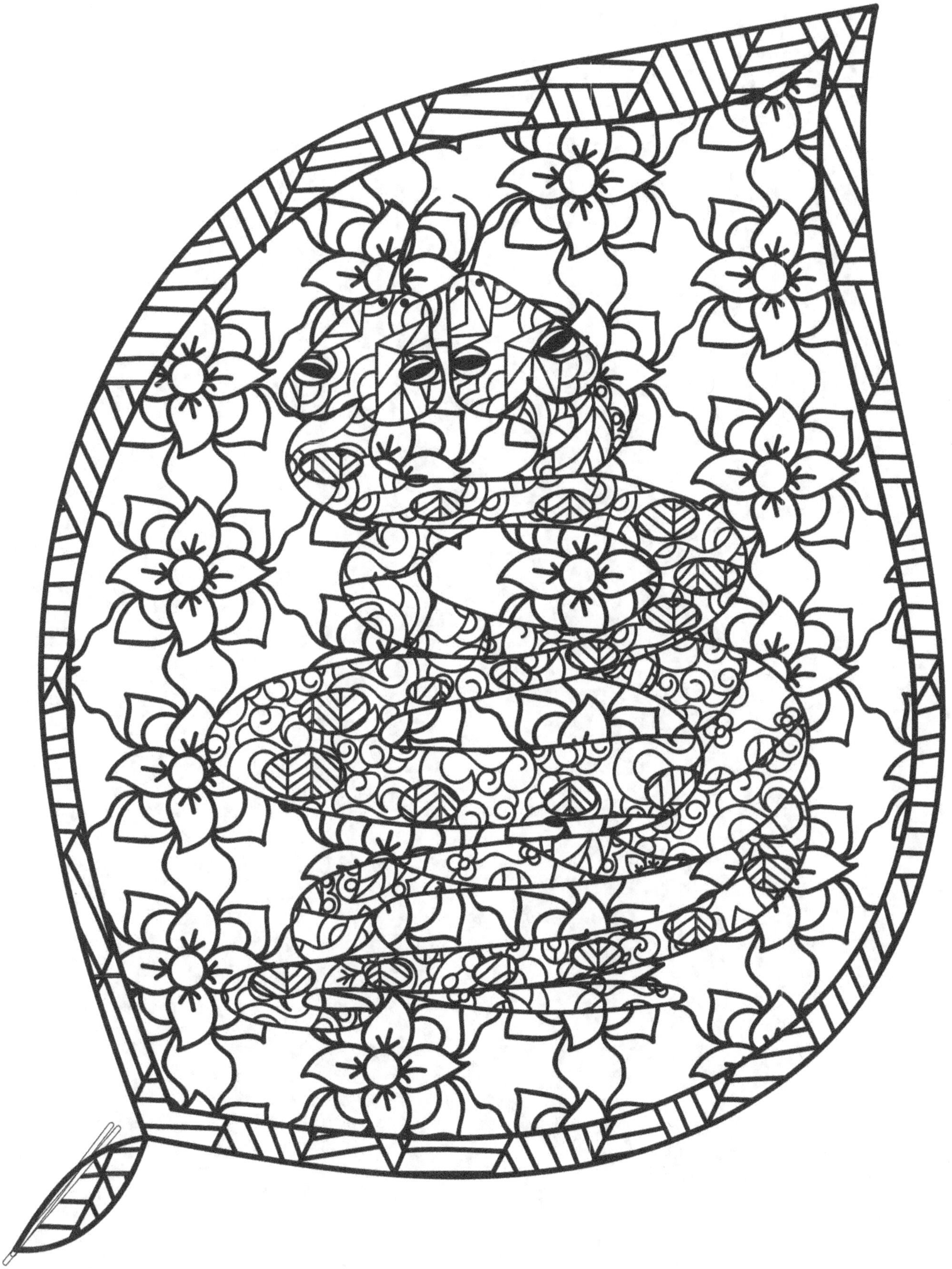

COLOR TEST PAGE

COLOR TEST PAGE